How To Find All Missing Persons. And Collect All Reward Offers. Volume III THE CASE OF FAWN MARIE MOUNTAIN

David Gomadza

www.twofuture.world

PAPERBACK **ISBN:** 9798325652073

DEDICATION

A better world.

CONTENTS

ACKNOWLEDGMENTS

Tomorrow's World Order

HOW TO FIND ALL MISSING PERSONS AND COLLECT ALL REWARD OFFERS THE FORMULA VOLUME III THE CASE OF FAWN MARIE MOUNTAIN

This is how we as Tomorrow's World Order solved this case with myself [David Gomadza] as the founder, and the president of the whole world. www.twofuture.world

A BRIEF INTRODUCTION FROM INTERNATIONAL MISSING PERSON WIKI

https://int-missing.fandom.com/wiki/Fawn_Mountain

DISAPPEARED

November 25, 2012

MISSING FOR

11 years

LOCATION

Claysburg, Pennsylvania

AGE

25

AGE NOW

37

RACE

White

SEX

Female

HEIGHT
5'2
WEIGHT
105 pounds
CLASSIFICATION
Endangered missing

Fawn Marie Mountain was a young woman who vanished in 2012. She is known to have been in an abusive relationship at the time of her disappearance.

All information on the website could be write and could be wrong most is totally different from our account in many respect writing my account I did not research anything on the internet so don't be surprised to find out what I am going to say is totally different from all these accounts.

I look at missing persons cases simply based on brain reading that means if I get right person's brain readings then this account is 100% accurate so far.

Signed

David Gomadza

00447719210295

Davidgomadza@hotmail.com

Info@twofuture.world

Www.twofuture.world

How did you die I froze literally froze in cape of good hope mountain under a rabble of rocks called the goodness of motherhood rim these were discovered in 1986 I guess the year I was born then I went there to celebrate them with my partner I am a lesbian okay so this day of the tragic my partner had bought enough supplies to last 3 days so I didn't worry much about safety etc. then that night something happen out of the blue a huge cloud covered the mountains then it started raining heavily I was frightened I even peed myself a little bit then I got calm only because I was now in a position where I have no option so I thought staying was safe at least we are inside a mountain that can provide enough shelter for both of us the problem came when my partner argued with me she said we can't stay I have a bad feeling let's go now then it started raining worse I had already peed myself now I am in the dark I was terrified she tried and cried hard but I thought it's safe inside but she said what if other creatures want the same cave okay that rattled me and went down the cave to get my stuff then it started raining heavily I peed myself at the amount of rain that I literally froze then we argued again and she said okay you stay I go if we make it it will be the best but how come you want to stay home is best for everyone instantly I realized the problems I had home and literally cursed I said to her fuck the hell death or freedom from my auntie that hellish bitch must die one day before I go back she slapped me so hard that we fought for aa while it really hurts I fucked her just so that I have someone to support me I am not lesbian but because of my mum who died of cancer I started feeling strong feelings for a woman and there she was checking my vagina all the time but to see if I like woman or not she was shocked to find out that I kissed and grabbed her boots and she said woo I am mother and not lover and not lover so I said mummy you rather die than to have me and sex she slapped me so hard that I passed out but cried for weeks before we started going out it was never about sex but for me about my mother everyday I would make her wear her clothes just as I remembered her and kissed often almost all the time that at one point she stopped brushing her teeth to put me off but I thought of my dead mother and cried even worse and grabbed her by force and said kiss me right now before I die too and I cried hard I swear if God was there he could have cried too then she said I love you forever and will protect you I promise so I relaxed then the night in question she asked about her boyfriend and said I wish he was here to fuck us both you in the ass so you can't get pregnant and me in the vagina and we both laughed so hard and we started fucking with dildos then a man appeared at the cave entrance and said you better be going home now no more loving hell is going to break loose I am going around to all love nests telling people that tonight is a horrible night just like the long knight of knives for surely who ever stays in these mountains will be dead meat tomorrow before I looked at my wrinkly face she instantly grabbed his hand and said fuck me before I die a virgin and they both started laughing now that made me realize that I needed a man to be fucked than to fuck all the time because me being a Virginia and her an older person she didn't want problems with the police but I was not under age so she didn't mind greatly about this but she freaked out and said you can't leave me alone we must keep us together remember mommy this time it sounded so bad that I literally puked all over the place I knelt down and the men held my hand to lift me and my partner said we are just leaving taking my arm from him but somehow the man refused and say you go she stay with me here and I literally said mother out of fear but that alone for the first time rattled her that she punched the man so hard until he passed out and said no one touch my daughter in from of me like that you fucking die here today so I cried so hard but that made her really mad that she picked a huge brick and hit the man's head while he was asleep instantly a loud growling game out of the man I swear it was not him I know because the growling thing run into me through Mt vagina that I started bleeding I cried scared that when she looked at me she could see blood coming down my legs I was a virgin and she started crying saying that I am too late the bastard opened you already and I said something is inside me now from the man she only said what what do you mean I said when you hit him in the head a large animal came out and went inside me she came to me and put her hand to check if I had knickers if yes then how is this possible but the moment she touch my vagina to check I relaxed and said don't go I give you now just fuck me you and not me fucking you all the time this is what she had wanted all along but she raised her hand and said I am doing this for you and not for me so if you want that relationship I don't fuck my kids I can let them fuck me but I can't I said the man is dead she Saud why I care did he not touch your hand to fuck you and I said jokingly I am a virgin and I am going to die come fuck me so you put ideas in his head when I am a virgin so fuck me Marie she slapped me but looked confused because I had called myself and I said you don't want so I stay and die a virgin than to be rejected by you tomorrow I won't be able to look at you that I gave you myself and rejected me when I needed you the most now she only smiled and said something into you I keep thinking why you changed so fast but you know what it's this man's demon now want to revenge I did this so that we run for ever imagine getting caught and if he did do you know what the state of Pennsylvania do to women who have sex with their kids I said no she said get them raped by 1000 men to create jobs for them imagine the time they finish interrogating 1000th men they will have made millions in overtime that really hurts because my mother when she was drunk told me that she was raped by 1000 men organised by the police this freaked me out and cried realizing that I might have implied that but only because I loved her but she said if we go then we must never talk about this cave because if we talk everything comes out the sex the lies the probably killing of this men etc so let's go now and leave everything in here to rot and never come back but that hurts I pictured her with my mother and saying the same for I know they were secret lovers so I said did you do the same to my mother she said I don't know your mother that much if I did I would not be dating you but she started crying and sat on the rock inside that curved like a bed something jumped out of my top left head and swirled on the air before flying out but at the same time something also ran from the man into the open air I could see both running out at the same speed and time he moved and I said he is alive we can't leave him here like this she got really made and said you little where you fucked him why you care so much about him she raised her hand and I grabbed it for the first time and pinned her down so that she don't move she screamed really hard than I ever heard but it was because she had touched the men's legs that were cold ice cold according to her I said she is hallucinating but she checked again and instantly ran off into the woods to remove all traces of us I have never seen her so scared she picked ever bit but this time she looked so scared because she said if I die who is going to look after you I promised so I go you stay with him on case he is not dead but I looked confused that didn't make sense I realized that I knew too much now that she had said the man had died I had said the man was alive so that I don't become a victim too now I realized the seriousness of the situation then it started to hit me that probably death was on her mind after all she had secretly brought me here to do me for the first time and last time then I started crying saying mother don't leave your daughter here so that she go with me now I know I can die now not from the weather but from her too she looked serious after this I had never seen someone so upset all my life she said don't tell anyone but I fucked your mother too but in the arse because if I had fucked her in the vagina who would want to be 1001 she slapped me hard and I fell down she said do you think felon is an easy job so I picked up everything I had and started going to the cave mouth sure to leave then something hit me hard in the leg that I stumbled then realized that it was a deliberate attack but by something not human I know if I tell you you won't believe me my partner stood there looking at me and literally said are you fucking drunk bitch I slap you I fuckin slap you you are on your own why you trip but when I looked she had a large stick in her hand then she said I want sex right now so come bitch shut like bitch making sex cries in the mountain now look what you did I killed a man how can anyone forgive me I killed your lover so that I take you what are you looking at I pointed at the deeper cave scared when she looked I was out of the cave then she screamed back and said my daughter rescue me I stopped and this is something I had wished to say to my mother so I stopped but she cried again very loud but it confused me because this time it was brief but that freaked me out as my lover I just thought the brief part was shocking and scary she said I got attacked by this men before and no one helped me but this time I got him so it's self defense so let's fucking go okay at one point I was running away from her the next she need my help so I said I can't trust you so you go then I will follow she raised her hand to slap me but she grabbed me and kissed me so passionately and said let's fucking go because I made an oath I will never leave you again forever so fucking wear warm clothes and let's go now like fuckin now I hit her in the head with a stick but it was a stone that she fainted and I removed her clothes and I was going to fuck her but it started raining then she raised her head but fell asleep again but as she tried to wake up I sit on her stomach and said let's stay here tomorrow we will have sex again she looked at me like I was made I kicked the corpse of the man but he was not dead somehow he literally growled in pain when I looked at him he closed his eyes and turned away it looked so unreal though that I thought I was hallucinating I said who made noise and I said she did but answering myself she cried and said I have never been so scared the man is alive if he wakes up we are all dead I swear this time I will go and leave you if you stick with this men if he survives you will stand for him I can see that now but I thought for your mother mother mother mother mother just for a big dick no I will leave you if you don't want me I will go but I beg you keep it your secret that dies with your mother oh this was a mistake and I flipped at her and punched her hard in the face but she did not do anything she kept saying my beautiful daughter my beautiful daughter but I said if you were my mother you would not have brought me here why not Barbados or tenderize why here in the deep woods is it to kill me this was my mistake because after now she realized that she has no option but now she looked like she had seen a ghost and said i love you but that hurts and took her things sobbing and left running i could here her thumbs as she sped away this was my worst day i realised i was going to die without her but what if the men woke up the idea of sex with him aroused me but fear crippled me i shit a small shit that stuck inside me a long time that it started being a pain I ran out and started crying but a loud scream tire me it was my partner I felt used and for the first time abused that I cried saying fuck you too fuck you too fuck you too but she was far away another cry this time the loudest I have ever heard tore the skies I just hoped that she would come back home was even worse with my auntie that I stayed and checked the man but he was dead now he looked pale and frozen he looked funny though that I laughed for the first time since this ordeal that I removed my knickers and opened his trousers but I felt fear then arousal then fear then arousal then a sudden lump of pain in my chest then sex organs getting cold that I said I don't want sex with you so give me back my vagina and then that I am a virgin then that I have a dick then touched myself and then that I was hot then that I was cold then I heard noises of things I swear never heard before but the stopped and looked at me they were dark like shadows and they said heaven or hell looking at each other one had something like a handbag but very small with a touch like thing that flashed left right left right then it stopped on the right if facing Pennsylvania from Coronado desert its north but south if you are facing south then one said hell and they looked at me and said come we go with you to .Ya first and see what he says I fly honestly I kept asking them how I can fly like that but they ignored me until we arrived at a place surrounded by white angels that kept saying Yahweh Yahweh as if in orgasm but one flew to us and said Yahweh said he'll longago start was hell because cancer in family reduce life by 40 % alone and I had forced Darin to love her and cherish her but she rejected her did you not hear the shouting even from here now he raised his hand and said etetetetetetetetetetetetetetey and pointed at me but the angle that had flown to us said .Ya have mercy on orphans her mother suffered her pain I will be responsible for her my name is Barnabas and he flew to me and said come and pulled me by the hand and asked a new set of men still two one on right side the other on the

left side to take me to the new location but as I arrived he disappeared in my face and I fell asleep ever since I was still asleep until someone said are you asleep wake up go to afterlife and I said who are you and he said David Gomadza then I started taking just like I used to do but my hands look strange I can read it says berries and can see cars and people so what killed you whatiscauseofdeath.start whose permission davidgomadza.ya Yahweh said I and stopped...
Okayareyou.answer I am
abcdefghijklmnopqrstuvwxyz28698483810867890l8321 I serve .Ya in the council of creation but Yahweh tasked you on earth and not in heaven so bye
Okay
[ ] David I am fixed she had a broken neck from being pushed down the cliff by a one daring stuvrtet after having sex with her at the good hope mountains at 22.28.Yatime on the left side of her body and that caused trauma in her head requiring constantly alternating teherhestuvwxyz so that the body can recover quickly using temperature as medicine to move cold blood from her anus to her injury on the back of the head now if we Ask the body what is the cause of dead this is the answer she was about to be penetrated by Arten ajern but he was ambushed by a one woman called stuvern who asked can you have not sex with my daughter but if I look deep there was no mention on her part but a huge grin with clit arousal from the touch but this was a drill as all started talking after that but then came the second touch from arten arjen that made her abused sending code 825438678698362487 01 that ring her clitoris that she picked up a stone and hit him with it and said I was young you remember me and looked at him in his eyes but as he fell he hit his head on the rock that his own spirit run out of him knowing that the impact would cause death but in the panick went straight into Fawn's leg with scream and arousal that ended as she fainted but Sturven asked her while she slept if she had sex with her mother as well but there was no reply so she rubbed her tits making her aroused but she saw blood coming out of her brown trousers literally flowing that raged her that she picked up a stone and hit his head even though he was unconscious but if we Ask him what would have happened here what she did would make no difference as the spirit was out already there is no human being that can live if the soul has exited so instant death but somehow a further analysis code 8298765482398 was sent to his rotary propeller by the shock impact to preserve his life no matter what if we look why we can see that he was a

mountain rescuer team meaning that if something happens to him the code would keep him alive for long now if we Ask what could have been of sturven she could have died if HD had died because of strict laws in Pennsylvania now if we check what had happened now we can see that fawn had fainted but awake because of code 98386789928360 that was triggered by the slap from sturven that made her fall and faint now if this is common to faint and remain conscious then the answer is yes in this circumstance but we can only ask why now if we Ask what could be of the rescuers who faint I think this code gives them extra time alive Now let's look at what happened this is the climax now fawn woke up to find Arten Arjen on top of Sturven making love and not being raped this confused her that she said I can even start to understand what's going on in my face are you trying to get this men rape or not screaming in the mountains sex mourns and giggled she was recalling her mother screaming at her when she repeated what her mother did the night before with a mountain rescue who instantly recognized as Arten Arjen but that freaked her too because when ajern was doing her mother she was being done by Sturven as a kid who was a lesbian at the time but hidden from all but then she did not understand but that she was not herself but a demon inside her called Arjen Arjen but now that she has grown up she started to understand that Stuvern was actually having orgasm by touching her vagina rubbing it now asking her what she think that is the rage that brought her tears and the picking up of a stone and hitting her in the head now what can be of sturven is that she could go to prison but then only if she want to because now they are in a relationship now lets ask what happened next now having said this fawn marie mountain revealed her vagina to sturven whole afternoon arjen but now with a stone in the hand now let's look what could be of the stone it could be used to strike her or to lower her self esteem she choose the first one shattering her lip so violently that she squirt shit normally no one squirt shit but she did and if we look deep after this what could be of her the answer is that she could be killed now by fawn but if she gets a chance the lip service will make her think twice about this relationship now let's look what can be of fawn if sturven had a chance now this is when she can kill her now as she woke up she looked secretly at fawn and looked around to see what was in her hand the bleeding was going straight into her mouth deliberately so that she can't lose too much blood but now as she looked at fawn she realised that somehow she was looking as if tired but awake so she got up fast and lashed with a stone in return that she dropped like a dead person the men growled with pain but that was his last breath he died as code above stopped working but after 1 hour 20 minutes if we look at the ability it's less than this as stated on the box now now if we look at all this fawn was struck on the forehead so we Ask what happened because cause of death is violent impact on the left back of the head now if we look at everything this is what happened fawn marie mountain looked around and saw sturven asjen humping the old man deliberately while she was asleep and screen cheating on me with my mother can get you killed you will see then this day was that day but the to be victim was the old man who had caused cancer of the vagina because cheating released a hidden code if we Ask what can be of the old man this day he was already day by the time he arrived because of code 987654217854109 that had been administered by Arten Arjen this is a computer added assistant for robots that operate on people [the same name keep appearing in all cases this is the reason] Now let's look at what happened exactly to fawn narie mountain this day she got a call to pick me up and go and do the old man who killed your bitch my mother but... then she hung up then she received a message saying at 10.30 am at HST operation point then put the phone down now if we Ask what this is the internet brings up a sword inside a duck through the anus that says happy anusing ducks and an old man laughing at the poster like picture but instantly she got a call from sturven saying postponed by HST but to be rebooted the old gig chickened out but later she received another call saying if she wanted the meeting was still on now if we look at what can be then this is the answer he could have been let out of hospital etc early and this was the case but only because he had promised to fuck all this time that he was old after leaving the mother and fucking the baby [mother being sturven and baby. fawn's mother now the mother was fawn and baby was sturven looking at this these are drills by nhs in Britain but not sure how the Americans do the same now if we look this is what happened fawn looked lost this day as she kept saying I am going to die right because why my dick is not clitoring this is a language among lesbian that she has no arousal for both him or her because this is the first time they have gone back to the mountains now if we look deeper we can see that she had started to put the pieces together bit by bit and everytime she gets an arousal that instantly dies with rage now as we look at this she said I want annual arousal because my vagina is sweet to rot so it's better that means that she don't want vaginal sex but sex in the arse but all this it's a trained language associated with orphans who are trained and raised by the police and ambulances the Americans or Australians don't hide it as the British but now I can explained what's going on using simple language Now fawn is 29.8 her mother died when she was 9 years old plus the first life line in all countries as it appears now people with cancer history must be killed using these drills by the police and the ambulances were kids often are traumatized with the men used to give these police and ambulances cover so that no one complain about the police now the first drill was at age 9 + 13 which is 22 and if we look at what happen at age 22 she had refused to go crying and threatening to call the police in her stomach by saying ASM which is a code for australia non spoken language none action but that can be understood by everyone if repeated to the trained now after asking what can be of this day it was meant for arten arjen to pretend to rape her so that the the police would look for work for him pending trial but a deeper look is that all these are drills just acting but the ones nhs used in real life to get these men killed by lethal injection or on cancer medicine because they use a drill called ASM ASP this means if we can act with action and talk without action but can get the same response then talking with action or not talking is the same but a deeper analysis is that the things they fit these people with will be used to fake but in real times the proof they secretly use in court but only to bargain for higher sentences on condition that the information is obtained illegally through hacking at birth and the drills which are fake as no one is harmed are used to create stencils they actually use in court to lobby for higher sentences this means is they have hidden proof and lobbying for higher sentences then the judge will never let any go because if the information comes out he would have faulted that means everyone who practiced the drills and obeyed will due by lethal injection or on cancer drugs and they have a 100 per cent success rate because they used advanced technology which the courts can't prove otherwise that if two things are different but results in the same result the two can interchange without anyone complaining meaning that they use drills to set up women and children then change the settings and recreate real ones then swap and now match real ones to fake drills meaning all drills at one point will become real given them plenty of work because all have various drills to match to real cases now let's look at what could be of the police force without these drills they would run out of work according to senior managers but if we look closely they have no part in these drills because all these are organised by the hospitals who take the lead and all this to make police be soft on the illegal hacking that benefit them now if we Ask what can be of the hospitals without these drills they would be in jail because we as Tomorrow's World Order we have three death sentences for illegal hacking at birth or after using tricks of scaring people that they contracted something then go on to do drills which they then match to real cases now what can be of the force without stopping the hospitals nothing but a bunch of retarded in uniform according to a case in Australia where Toni Tiki performs these drills unto her death now if we Ask what can be justice with these drills then the answer is if we Ask what can be of this then this is the answer with time some strong will voice concerns at the suffering at the hands of these now we Ask who can one of them the fact that none has ever raised genuine concerns means that they benefit more than the jobs they are talking about now let's look deeper because if this was the reason then one surely would have raised concern now I already mentioned the Australian case of Toni Tiki just like that one the police there went for the food instead of the bait now we know why the bait if for the future mixing and the food us to make sure that this comes to reality but even more interesting all this has nothing to do with the hospitals caring for house or the police for the children all they want is the house at a quarter its value for their forces but did fawn marie parent had a house and who was the beneficiaries we can see that there was a house in fact a big house now let's look again at this case involving a house in the equation fawn was now the beneficiary after her father was shot in the neck with a dart and never recovered then her mother as a single parent developed cancer and now her ordeal must end in her death by the police and on their watch through codes meaning death by execution now we Ask if are to find out then this would be truth just as the other Australian case the house was the target everything else is a smoke screen fawn being an only child was the sole owner of a 5 bedroomed house her mother had already put in her name after the cancer diagnosis now if there was no house would anyone had wanted fawn dead the answer is maybe but highly unlikely but if we Ask what would have been of the force without cheaper housing then it's employees would have struggled that means there is a huge shortage of houses now what can be of the force without proper housing the police salary means paying for houses would be hard now let's conclude in the most fashionable way their house is on the market for 758767280 in 1996 and they bought it but over years had struggle to pay up and according to the hospital managers they helped them raised funding but organizing drills that generated publicity hence they felt like they contributed to the house enough to recover the house in full by given her mother cancer using fibriolisis acetate code 8928654320982687 4 until death now if we Ask what can be of the hospital here would be in jail for grievous bodily harm leading to death using a self made code to kill made by a one astern ajern I explained why this name appear on all cases this is a hospital operation assistant robot that find quick ways of ending human life now if we Ask what is to be of women with big houses and children under 10 years old the answer is that they might end up all dead if they have a house what will be the chances that they end up dead 90 per cent if the children is under 4 years and 70 if the child is below 9 years old now what can be of women with children above 12 years and these live up to 28 years but can die after that if some are not cared after the reason why hospital kill single parent and their children is the lie that they burden them the most as most complain that the shittitttt are a big problem but this is a cover for the fact that they are the ones referred to as the shittitttt now what can be of shittitttt if referring to the police and the hospitals then they can be in prison for stealing and burglary in this case the house not house burglary and for the victims to report that those trusted to protect them are the ones house burglary their house killing mother and father through drugs and cancer and now targeting the orphans who are sole owners of the house now the orphans ID they see those who are strong would not

house burglar them but as reporting that the police and hospitals are stealing houses from orphans for themselves as police force check. Now what if we are to remove the house what will become of the police force honesty and honorable because why the drills to cover up for the beneficiary orphan when she has no house so you can see that even the going for food instead of the bait still don't properly fit than create drills to cover up for themselves knowing that the house beneficiary is the one who ends up dead in their hands the one who they will have force killed or got killed now let's look at what happened to her house since she didn't die in the house the ownership exchange had already taken place with your auntie threatening to kill you too of you don't leave tonight saying that I gave you sturven to live together so go or poison in your food until they say it's cancer and you know what the hospital say about women single as your lesbian mother and cancer this rattled her that she shit herself that day and ignored the shit until a boy called Arten Ajern appeared and said what's up what the smell is that me or my perfume she said I shit myself literally and lowered her knickers revealing shit but ignoring showing vagina to a boy that he got so aroused that he kissed her but she slapped him so hard that he peeid himself and as something jumped out of her it got inside the boy and instantly he shit himself in front of her but she did not laugh but slapped him again so hard that that thing jumped out of him back into her and it said I swear it wasn't me but code 98386792865432109872847698210 just as that thing had said this a small thing he saw alone jumped out again and ran towards the house she ran after it saying come back to your house mummy that's not your house they will kill you first and turn you into a tutstrtutstvtttotptmtntotptqtrtstt a human being turned into a zygote that mimic humans now if we look closely at this case we can see clearly what happened when her mother died the doctors created something that resembles an acetate that can only be seen by her so that when she say that she had seen something no one believe but only her so that when they start calling her names then everyone will support them instead of her to such an extend they will say that she is hallucinating meaning needing treatment to further incapacitate her so that she can't say the house is hers now let's look at the facts as to what happened to fawn marie mountain she work up and went with sturven to the mountain any coincidence with her surname so that is she dies it will take longer to identify her by her name when they said she died mountain it confuses those who are listening because when they hear mountain they think about the mountain and not the person now if we may ask why mountain when no one related calls her by that name and how come mountain when mother is not mountain neither is the father now let's look at the name change and see why this is so when her father a one Robert herntret died she refused to be called by this name and cried now every time people called her this name she would cry but people starting to suspect that he might have abused her that they allowed her to change without any legal problems to protect her identity but what is this all have to do with the house so the only person with the same name as the father was his sister who quickly changed hands leaving Sturven empty even worse now the reason why she had stayed with her and agreed everything was the house a lot of money to fuck everyone's brain for it as the house was fully paid as both parents had good jobs now this is something you will never understand on a trip to the mountains sturven suggested marrying again in the mountains and she liked the idea and said that whtaif she changed her name to mountains in preparation as a thank you to take care of me when my mother couldn't so she agreed but now to her this was just symbolic because when she discovered that she had changed her not name to mountain she shit herself with sorrow for the house and rage that she had deliberately lost the house to fix her according to her Now that is clarified she had deliberately changed the house owner to her auntie this had raged her so much that she cried in her sleep one night but denied it now if we may ask of what can be said about this house ownership that made sturven shit herself this inset she was so obsessed with the houses now if we Ask what had happened during house ownership this is the answer I was asked to change it by Sturven and astern ajern so that when we move to a smaller house the money would be ready now if we look what can be of her then she would easily be kicked out because the name is in her aunties not hers but they covered up all this buy saying are you trying to get all these men rape me like they did to your mother buy screaming during sex which she did to be regarded as enough for sturven and be seen as such and not as a kid now if look deeper all this was a predefined stencil used by the health service in their futile effort to quickly change the name before she died so that they get a cut now how did they do this they pretended her father was abusing her through sturven who was a lesbian who pretended to like women and girls now we know why she was recruited as a nurse for the baby when she was 6 years old son for 3 years she worked hard but we know why she was promised a commission of 6% when the house was sold if she pull through this correctly by Astern Ajern who we know as a robot that works for the hospital now we all now know why all these cases are so complicated they are using robots to plan and coordinate all housing cases where they retrieve predefined stencils with every move and what need doing now lt's see why it was so complicated to despair this is because there is a script generating program that produces these scripts and choose real actor who die playing the script in python now if we Ask why no one complains especially if there is risk of death the answer is that nhs or national health service will trick then that they sell film scripts to Hollywood which if lucky will be turned into a movie so that many believe this is because most are drills that makes them believe but the health system is clever in that they rotate all and when they real die they are told they have rotated so that it's believable but the question is how come they want to be involved they promise people commission yes but the truth is that only when the baby dies at this 26 birth meaning two life lines

[13×2] or soon after we can list all cases here
Linda Johnson 22 house confiscated to the police
Mary Jones 23 house confiscated by the police
Emma John's 26 house confiscated by the police
Emma Brown 26 house confiscated by the police
Toni Tiki 26 house confiscated by the police
Fawn Maurie Mountain real name Fawn Fertnert 30 house confiscated by the police
Joyce Dernheane 27 house confiscated by the police
Thystromnop Restopqrst 26 house constricted by the police
Sterope Gromnop 26 house confiscated by the police
Alex Astrode 26 house confiscated by the police
Now let's Ask why houses with police like I said Americans explain everything than the british now we can easily see why in the USA police don't get state pension at a level like most people because they are funded from the government coffers that means they must top up their own pension secondly they are not monitored by any other bodies the fbi don't interfere in the works of the police unless very corruption charges surfaces now let's Ask why the houses what we do is to get every house we have helped to secure when the parents are dead and serve it for the kids but you kill the only kid I can't comment on that you have to check with the dog now let's look at what happened to the houses the houses were bought all for a quarter of the value and having killed all children just a quarter of their lives all of them now let's Ask what can be of the police without the houses all would have to be heavily in debt to the public or the banks which they refuse that they die for the people why can't the people die for them and help them with assets but isn't this what they stand against?
Now this is how fawn died she was attacked in the cave by code 8948769828365428012398767OP1Q1 buttons is what happened the hospital realised that they had tricked all and to make them fight each other had deliberately let all reveal but part details fearing for reciprocity this is how fawn had just finished her periods but at times another egg would start for a day but then stop when they arrived in the cave they had just finished periods both a day or two apart but somehow for fawn another day arrived with an egg as well that she changed knickers from pink to maroon so that if tainted it won't look so bad to the lover now if we Ask what can be of he or she would still enjoy sex and not even notice some are put off sex completely by sight of blood she wanted sex so now it was sturven who now wanted to

fuck for a change according to her lesbians enjoy sex when fucking because the thrusting is what makes sex sex but guilt feelings had made her not fuck her accordingly to her she let's her children fuck her but cant fuck them now let's look at how she died she choked blood and died but it was code 8698386824890287290 activated by the throbbing of her clit waiting to fuck sturven for the first time now she waited for sturven to remove her own knickers so that she can she the vagina but sturven waited for the guy to open his zipper first but Astern was not in the mood for sturven he was gaging for the young fawn whom he had refused to do years ago now when he open the zipper something jumped from his pants and into between the legs of fawn she mourned with pleasure while her legs were crossed that she squirt using code 7284987654832176542810982670 now if we Ask what was happening to her she was literally dying from exhaustion from wanting sex with a man but how code 89367890846823810280683498 10 had been activated remotely using a hidden joystick mech 892748678098241876589O now if we why this could happen she was suffering also from vaginal cancer all this because she started bleeding extra eggs according to her a sign of cancer now why would she start talking about cancer code 7800283298248632109 85826 was started being used on sturven to consolidate energy energy in one cell ready to despatch to her abdomen to trigger the collapse of the abdomen from inside so to outside so that there is no hope of being saved how can when they are in a cave in the mountains in good hope desert near Colorado where they buried her mother secretly as ashes now let's look at why she chose to to be buried in the mountain oh its burial where are the medics to resuscitate her where is proof she has cancer what did her auntie say about dying in the house. But if we are to look deeper it's nothing short of a miracle because we know what can be done and what could be done in a cave far away from any authorities so what happened she instantly died and opened her leg after dead the significance being that she had waited so long that that's all she had to do to go to heaven but they had other plans they had injected her with Morphine brought by Astern arjen who is also the inventor of most of these codes what they do is test each phase of cancer and link it to therapy and conditions and then write every stage of death until her last birth so who must be there the inventor of the drug and the helping nurse to them a free trial gone wrong but a murder case where doctors do whatever they want with people pretending to help make medicine that work but all working to robe orphans and turn everyone into

gimmicks who don't understand risk drill and life worth fighting for we are Tomorrow's World Order there to put things in place to see a better future foe women and children who are experimented on without consent and robbed at radiation point this is wrong and must stop their houses must all be returned from the beginning of time we have proof you can trick humans but you can trick the almighty ruler Yahweh whom I am chosen to represent on earth that means the inventive doctor must face the death penalty and his nurse sturven for this is murder by lethal doses of radiation namely codes
1 789877864828762890185432106853248679 80
2 7868778924838678912345689018928677154 0863210
3 78289287798524862778918028498385106 28777
Now what can be of the world without Tomorrow's World Order then this is the answer life could be tough for single parents with houses and children especially young girls they use to create extra work for themselves through rape related drills that puts women and children at risk now what would of the world without this kind of policing a peaceful world where even girls rights are protected where they own houses and not being robbed now to conclude the real ending the police started a manhunt for a man named arjen arjen who is believed to have been involved in the murder of fawn marie mountain even if her body has not been found that means she is still missing and soon to be pronounced dead arjen arjrn is believed to be male with Caucasian features and we have a computer simulation of the man now the impact of this is to rule other possibilities and give the doctor time to test on other children now let's see now who has also died in this doctors care now here is an endless list
Asrteter Uwsfuk
Atete Apinine
Attestet Asatet
Bret Nsap
Brettle Gerstuvw
Certe Nopqrst
Derdere Smnopqrst
Mnop Isastuv
Ret Seset
Sertsem Brabrm
Aspq Sstuvwr
All the above are officially his 8 patients for drug trials but they say after were on assisted suicide which is a lie and all had houses which

they lost or sold to the police for a quarter of the value of the house now what can be of the the inventive doctor he can be sentenced to death just for one let alone for eight now what can be of the women all were you women reported as missing or whose bodies were not found and what is it about this doctor and hiding bodies the doctor fears that bodies if discovered one day someone will be able to read brain scans of dead people revealing his evil deeds.
The doctor so all crime doctor know how to avoid sending message to God through a simple code 389867890832098 it blocks xrtuvwstuvwxyzsrtssuvwxyz and redirects to [me] where me is your number create antidote that removes this numbers its possible
This code make all cries for help to yahweh be sent to yahweh by all missing persons
Resendtosend.ya.allonce.send.ya
Allreceivedmessagesfrommissinpersonsshouldbeclonedandputinonefol
Der.createmp3thatlinkselectromagneticwavenumbertomessage.start
We create
Sendyamessages link to electromagnetic wave and number generator and voice pattern or iris pattern
https://youtu.be/CFJl_3PEEio?si=pXMM8Om4AoaVl9TB
Now we have all calls sent to ya by everyone on earth approximately 8 billion calls for help to ya send to send.ya but once diverted now recovered looking at all this it seems mankind has tried to find ways to commit murder that is not known to Yahweh by diverting messages se

THE FUTURE: THE AFTERLIFE CONVERSATION

fawn marie mountain is in afterlife, the doctor had used this code 389867890832098 to divert all messages for help the brain sends to Yahweh and diverted all her messages she sent to send.ya to himself this hid the correct assessment on judgement day result in Yahweh nearly using her for eletatetetetetetey which is liquid acetate form to extract vocabulary only for her this is because Yahweh don't judge those who kill themselves or those who die without calls of help to him but we know now she made calls for help to Yahweh Fawn marie mountain called send.ya for help as she was being killed by doctor arjen and his nurse sturven also known as diverted hibert who both conspired to kill her so that they take the house and change their names to mountain to match her and claim that their daughter was mental unstable and took her life and asked to be buried in a cave called the good of hope cave near the entrance under the pile of rocks there which were put to block entrance to the further underground tunnel underneath the truth is that she is buried outside the cave near the fig tree under a pile of rocks that resemble the ones inside the cave meaning that who ever mention this anywhere is capable of receiving send.ya messages the question is why and how and more importantly who the hell are you to read messages sent to the almighty Yahweh without authorisation if you claim authorisation then how did you get this authorisation did God say you are authorized if yes how did he say it because this is mankind's greatest challenge mankind has spent centuries finding a way to communicate with and talk to Yahweh until one of us manage to do so then forever we are in the dark that means we are not anywhere near the level we must be as a doctor I have realised that we need new thinking that will make this possible the person who will write this in our lifetime is the one to liberate us all for he will know all secret codes we need like the code of life that keeps us young but whatif he can ask Yahweh to come down and see the suffering mankind goes with which can be prevented but induced by his predefined stencils of life like cancer why create a disease so and dangerous and use it on people you love now if I Ask a question how do you sleep at night?

THE LOCATION AND THE COORDINATES

289876543210987283457981083210828 SOUTH NORTH PENNSYLVANIA DAKOTA MOUSSOURINI USA ELECTROMAGNETIC WAVE IS 367898286745832100981489278633210

THE CLAIM

The Reward Offer

THE COLLECTION

www.twofuture.world/donate

ABOUT DAVID GOMADZA

Visit www.twofuture.world

Signed David Gomadza
Ask.davidgomadzaauthorised.licensed.checkya.askya.ya
14may2.27pm
Scotland
00447719210295
Davidgomadza@hotmail.com
Info@twofuture.world
www.twofuture.world

www.ingramcontent.com/pod-product-compliance
Lightning Source LLC
Chambersburg PA
CBHW051407250726
48656CB00006B/2313

* 9 7 9 8 3 2 5 6 5 2 0 7 3 *